Dazzling
DIGGERS

For Kate, Tim, ...ry and Angus - T.M.

First published 1997 by Kingfisher
This edition published 2013 by Macmillan Children's Books
an imprint of Pan Macmillan,
a division of Macmillan Publishers Ltd
20 New Wharf Road, London N1 9RR
Associated companies throughout the world
www.panmacmillan.com

ISBN: 978-1-4472-1265-2

Text copyright © Tony Mitton 1997
Illustrations copyright © Ant Parker 1997
Moral rights asserted.

5 7 9 8 6 4

A CIP catalogue record for this book is available from the British Library.

Printed in China

Dazzling
DIGGERS

Tony Mitton and Ant Parker

MACMILLAN CHILDREN'S BOOKS

Diggers are noisy, strong and big.

Diggers can carry and push and dig.

Diggers have shovels to scoop and lift,

blades that bulldoze, shunt and shift.

Diggers have buckets to gouge out ground,

breakers that crack and smash and pound.

Diggers move rubble and rocks and soil,

so diggers need drinks of diesel oil.

Some have tyres and some have tracks.

Some keep steady with legs called jacks.

Tyres and tracks grip hard as they travel,

squish through mud and grind through gravel.

Diggers go scrunch and squelch and slosh.

This dirty digger needs a hosepipe wash.

Diggers can bash and crash and break,

make things crumble, shiver and shake.

Diggers can heave and hoist and haul.

Diggers help buildings tower up tall.

Diggers park neatly, down on the site.

Then digger-drivers all go home. Goodnight.

Digger bits

levers

these control different
parts of the digger

tyre

this helps the wheel to
grip the ground and get
the digger moving

bucket

this is for digging
and scooping out

jack

this holds the
digger steady when
it is lifting or digging

piston

this is a strong pump
that makes parts of
the digger move about

breaker

this is for cracking
concrete or lumps
of rock

blade

this is for knocking
down and pushing along

tracks

these help the digger
to travel over slippery
or bumpy ground